W9-CLN-963

Boys Whistling like Canaries

Boys Whistling like Canaries

Jorn Ake

EASTERN WASHINGTON UNIVERSITY PRESS

Front cover photograph: Jorn Ake, *Boots: Prague* (2002)
Back cover photograph: Alyssa Salomon, *Canary, Male*, cyanotype (2007)
Cover and interior design by Erin T. Dodge.

Library of Congress Cataloging-in-Publication Data
Ake, Jorn, 1964–
   Boys whistling like canaries / Jorn Ake.
     p. cm.
   Poems.
   ISBN 978-1-59766-050-1 (alk. paper)
   I. Title.
   PS3601.K39B69 2009
   811'.6—dc22

                    2008054035

The paper used in this publication meets the requirements of ANSI/NISO
Z39.48-1992 (Permanence of Paper).

Eastern Washington University Press
Spokane and Cheney, Washington

Contents

Four Angels

6

Four Voices

8

I got sick and tired of all that purity—
I wanted to tell stories.

—Philip Guston

1

Atlas Ptáků

This morning the bird arrived with the wrong colors
more beautiful in the Prague outside the window
than in the book full of pictures with wrong names.
I tried to watch my language at the kitchen table
without losing sight of my tongue.
My wife said I needed lessons and some money
to be happy at a bookstore with some coffee.
I thought only about my tongue's depression.
The birdseed washed away with the rain
but the bird came back again and again,
returning to the continental tree
from the island window ledge,
another's bell voice counting the trips out loud.
The magpie arrived on the chimney
and called down his ř-ř-ř-ř-ř-k
that I could not make with my tongue.
My wife was being right in Bratislava,
then Budapest and finally at a dam on the river Danube
where wetlands were more unfortunate.
I could not say what I saw.
I was looking through binoculars
at a country with a history of oppressive lenses.
The language was my fault.
Still, when the falcon flew over
the birds fled no matter what name I used,
and the lady in the window of the other building
waved to me or at me or just away from herself.

Outside, It's America

America is in a way the inability to think of gold metaphorically.
        —John Fowles

Prague, 1969

Torch #1 careens across the street towards the Museum,
his skin popping, the pain so intense
even bystanders feel their fingernails peel
and the voice in their spine scream

run

run

the flames a man
eating another man

as he fights to get out of the burning car
of himself before it explodes,

his lungs boiling and he falls
to be smothered, to be extinguished,

as a gold ring slips
from his skinless hand.

Křivoklát, 1952

When just ten years after Terezín
they hang Slansky

his father leaves for the country
and the little house along the Beroun
with the crooked door and crooked chair,

where the alchemist,
one-legged and desperate,
jumped from Emperor Rudolf's
goldless dungeon,

and waits in the dark
for them to come get him

again,

their black Tatra gliding
along the ash-wet streets

like the alchemist's ghost
come back to reclaim his orphaned shoe.

Kladno, 1948

A miner pries a small pebble of gold
from a seam in the rock

and keeps it
to himself.

Thus begins the worker's paradise.

From this day forward
history is his fault.

Natalka

Our cleaning lady in Prague is slender and muscled

and she pushes me away from the sink
with a finger pointed towards my office
where she knows I write

poezii. Uklízet budu já.
poetry. I will clean.

She is from Ukraine, where men kill other men

with industrial toxins and old oil heaters
rigged to fill a house with carbon monoxide,

a death as gritty as black & white newsreel
of a python crushing an antelope
on the floor of a silent jungle in the 1930s.

But these men do not do dishes and she
is not from a jungle—she is from Ukraine
and speaks Czech with a strangeness
that makes my neighbor cluck *hrozně*, horrible,
her mother tongue mangled by foreigners

as I sweat through my entire vocabulary
just to tell Natalka thank you, give her money,
and ask about the thirteen-year-old daughter
she hasn't seen in eight months.

She says, "*Nemůžu nic dělat. Volám jí a říkám ´Miluji tě´
a ona na to ´Pošli peníze.´*"

"I can do nothing. I call her and I say, 'I love you,'
and then she says, 'Send money.'"

Unspoken, that thirteen-year-old girls are
an export commodity in Ukraine—

Natalka and her husband are another,

she a schoolteacher cleaning houses and he
a chemist laying brick,

working more cheaply by half than any Czech
but making more in six months than a whole year in Ukraine.

Meanwhile their daughter's body starts to hum like a hive,
the swarm gathering energy inside her

just like any teenager in any shopping mall in America
except that she is in Ukraine

chaperoned only by a grandmother with bad hips
who doesn't understand cell phones or music television

or Kyev, where anyone with money and contacts
can buy a thirteen-year-old girl with cash
and take her to Prague, Belgrade, Tel Aviv, Dubai—

but she is not in Dubai, she is in Ukraine
and her mother, Natalka, is in my kitchen

one finger pointed towards my office
or standing in the hall one hand on her hip

while I stammer weather and nice day and birds
and she says work visa and mafia, meaning

she works nine months to make six months' salary
and buy back her passport with three months'

to spend the remaining three
in Ukraine—

until she's back again and I meet her
shopping for sponges with friends,

four Ukrainian women as slender
and muscular as she

and she tells them:

To je můj šéf.
On je básník.
Z Ameriky.

Here is my boss.
He is a poet.
From America.

And they smile and look at me sweetly,
as if I were an endearing but slightly dim child,

and say without saying, *This is not poetry.*
This is what we make for ourselves out of life.

Rain Coming Down like a Death of Angels

When Heisenberg met Bohr in 1941, two boys in Indiana
were trading marbles like atoms in a dirt lot beside the barber shop
where their fathers were busy getting their hair cut,

agate desirable for its ability to crack glass in half
like a melon with a machete on an island in the Pacific.

One of these boys would lose his father
and one of them would not, changing each
in ways American English was not equipped to handle,

its
be a man
and
say what you mean

a paradox as stable and uncertain
as the wavy patterns in the agate marble

one boy holds up to his eye
while the other doesn't say anything at all

like
Isn't it beautiful?
or
I love the way the fiery red cuts through the blue,
don't you?

Black sticks of the trees looking over their shoulders
as each marble is named and counted

Black Lightning. Green Arrow.

Fat Man. Little Boy.

Two nights ago a wonderful northern light was visible,
the whole sky was covered with green rapidly changing veils,

the loveliest marble holding a secret fissure
cut through from the black & red

invisible but audible
once bounced on the pavement
like a click in the jaw
after grinding teeth during sleep—

one boy full of the future
as dark as heavy water

the other so certain he's picking out patterns—

^{235}U plus a neutron yields ^{141}Ba, ^{92}Kr, and 3 free neutrons,

but what to do with all the leftover energy?

In Berlin we had pouring rain, over Neustrelitz
storm and rain showers as if from buckets,
in Rostock it cleared up,
from Wenemunde on the sky was scrubbed clean.

The boy looks at the marble with the crack
in its eye and thinks he'd trade even
two for one, the beauty as unspeakable
as his desire for it, sweaty in the fall chill

with the fever of ownership, of mastery,
layered over the sweet core of weakness

that leads the hand to slide through an opening
in the clothes of another sleeping innocently on a bench.

Which boy knows and which boy learns
about the crack in the marble

and who finds the other
suddenly missing from school,
chair empty, house darkened,

a hole in the ground where his father used to be?

Over the next twenty years, Bohr writes
ten careful letters he does not mail.

Each one goes something like this:

Dear Heisenberg,
Two boys are trading marbles.

One marble is cracked.
One boy knows.

Only the marble
cannot be blamed.

Operation Anthropoid

—May 27, 1942

Her mother said go outside please and move that bicycle
she thought of the boy down the street

humming to herself and herself only
moved the bicycle around to the back

he had blue eyes and blond hair and said
strange things about his father

the bicycle so heavy
but the handgrips warm

remember please move it around to the back
remember to remember to remember

to go around the back quickly

will you remember

who could forget the boy
the blue eyes even hungry and alone

her mother pulled from the dead
after she pulled for herself

the bicycle

the handgrips were still warm
the eyes still blue

the butcher of Prague dying
from his wounds in a hospital bed.

In Which Freud Leaves Vienna and Goes Instead with Moses to London

We cannot imagine our own death, and when we attempt to do so, we can perceive that we are in fact still spectators.
    —Sigmund Freud

Before they could all go completely insane,
the people of Vienna had first to expel Freud
into the Sinai by train to Paris—

the difficulty not in the execution of the deed
but in the doing away with the traces.

Freud as old as Moses and full of holes, his mouth
gutted by cigars burned like one bush after another
dropped through a broken skylight,
ash sooting the air as it falls—

one dream involving the river turning into blood
and one dream involving swarms of frogs.

The maid chases a hooded crow from the hall banister
with a wire rug-beater, and the bird clangs off the transom
then out through the double windows at the landing,
its feet raking the coppered sill like a scorpion scuttling a can.

How unaware the neighbors are on purpose!

Of this Jew who named desire's darkest bulb
mother, as in the boy loves his mother to death
and is led like a lamb to her flame.

That a word could be a light so blinding

friends shall make war on friends like enemies,
and the earth and those who inhabit it shall be terrified—

Hitler rising from the smoke to the west,
and Freud wondering what makes him
not Moses,

wondering what makes Moses
not Hitler, not Freud—

the conception of a god 'choosing' a people,
making it 'his' people and himself its own god.

When the photographer comes each evening,
he carries only the small leather bag of a doctor,
two cameras, both German made,
and no more than just enough film for his work—

let none of it remain until the morning,
anything that remains until the morning you shall burn

documenting everything in its place

now that everything is guilt,
everyone up to something no good,

like filling in the blanks for exit visas to promised lands—

everywhere in the Empire, the temples were closed,
the services forbidden,
and the ecclesiastical property seized—

chosen people facing chosen people
every day in the streets,

separated and sorted
by who chose them for what
and in what percentages.

But can a single person create a new religion so easily?

The maid stands at the window, watching
as the crow screams out her location,
a trickle of sweat figuring her temple,
her nipples tightened as if in clamps—

Heiss. Kalt. Juden.

They've labeled the street like a public shower,
the city awash in a hysteria of narrative—

a door not a door until a swastika hangs above it—

the bushes not God until burning.

What progress we are making. In the Middle Ages
they would have burnt me; nowadays
they are content with burning my books.

The photographer sits waiting in the entry,
nervously shuffling and reshuffling his film.

The maid retreats to the kitchen
where she prepares a paste Freud can eat.

The plague of crows stays outside, the one
joined by three more, multiplying each other,
none remembering who was the first.

For what are we, that you murmur against us?

Little souls hung from the tree like a gang of spirits
in floppy black & white pajamas. Until finally,

the maid throws out a husk of bread from the breakfast
and they fall silent and tumble upon it and themselves—

the gingerman running from children bent
on his destruction, the Viennese trying on bodies
they desire more than their very own—

Ach, du warst in abgelebten Zeiten
Meine Schwester oder meine Frau

people broken apart and loose on the streets

every man his brother, and every man
his companion, and every man his neighbor

even God seems to confuse who is who
unless marks are made on the jambs,

and Freud has a cigar not a sword or a staff,
his pen no mightier than Moses
listing his fears from the couch:

Reichsfluchtsteuer
Steuerunbedenklichkeit
Judenvermogensabgabe

the words grown so long against the Jews
as if escape were made impossible purely by size.

Over 31,000 Reichsmarks for the old man!
But his sisters, Freud's four great sofas of fabric
knitting below in the garden—those ladies are priceless!

The maid weeps at the sink into a hand towel.
The photographer takes a few shots of the hat
lingering on the rack, the spare stick waiting.

You shall not bear false witness against your neighbor.
You shall not covet your neighbor's house.

People will be so many things,
no one will remember who they were.

Freud says: *Deep within me, there continues to live*
the happy child from Freiberg.

Moses says: *Your lamb shall be without blemish.*

A cloud of smoke in his tabernacle skull,
a spot of blood on his doorstep—

So he let him alone

to wonder whether the evil Moses met

at a lodging place on the way

could be so easily man-made now.

Are you not a bridegroom of blood to me?

To receive an answer, first

pay $2,000,000 for an old man
who'll die in a year,

and lose four sisters
in Terezín, Treblinka, and Auschwitz
6,000,000 times,

then take the hat from its hook
the stick from its tree

and with the armies of Pharoah
charging behind you
part the Red Sea.

At Břeclaw, the Train Meets the Border

≈

1938 (going north)

Stopped at the border,
the train reversed.

A few jumped and ran
forever
into the black-wooded marshland.

There were shots,
but no one saw them fall.

Everyone else died in the camps.

≈

1988 (going south)

Stopped at the border,
all the Czechs leave.

The guards and their dogs
stare hard at everyone left.

You are afraid they see something
you do not even know about yourself.

Like they will last forever.

≈

2004 (going nowhere)

Stopped at the border,

a fat old woman and her retarded grandson
squeeze into seats facing yours,

his eyes so lovely and wet
they reflect the fall trees back at you

like two worlds swimming
in pools of flaming gasoline.

They take forever
wherever they go.

Near the end, we met to plan political actions. Secret police everywhere. When one meeting is finished, we would pick the place for next meeting. So no one knew. Of course we had spy. Maybe neighbor through the wall. Or lady on the street with broom, sweeping and sweeping. One of us could be it. We don't know. It could be anybody, that's the thing. But last meeting, we go to the house near where Hrabal—you know him? great writer—fell from window. Maybe jumped. Anyway. When we finish, we leave one by one so no one gets suspicious. But we look down to the street and no one comes out of ground floor. Second man goes and no one. Third. Same. We know then they must be on first floor waiting.

Who?

Secret police! They are there, arresting people on first floor, putting them in basement. Holding them there. That's why no one comes out. And you know what is strange? We keep going down. One by one. Why did we do that? No guns with these men. We could run away. Easy. We all go downstairs together, maybe they get one or two but others can run away. Why not run? Why did we just let them take us?

You had family. You didn't want them to do anything to your family.

No, no, that's not it. I can't explain it to you. I can't explain it to myself. We were so stupid. Even when we had this unity, still so far apart. So divided. From each other. From our self. They were everywhere, even our heads. You don't think you can escape when you cannot escape by thinking.

Then what happened?

They kept us maybe two hours. Then let us go. I think I was only one who wasn't spy. Funny, yes. In a way, I felt ripped off. I think maybe I should get paid also for this. You know, like the others. Instead of being dissident for free, you know? But I do not. Maybe wife will kill me. And I am glad, but what is this government now we have? Democracy? Democracy of bastards maybe. Instead of taking us, they just take our money. Pardon me, but they are bastards, that is right word, yes?

Losing the World Championships

Crowds welcoming Hitler. Look at the crowds.
The crowds—that's how it looked.
There's a stranger.

—Anna Freud (video commentary, Freud Museum, Vienna)

The pole-vaulter is touching what he had planned on missing. I can see when he realizes he cannot stop what comes afterwards, his small world of the bar slipping from its supports to hover briefly above the large world below. He has lost his space, and yet time is unfinished with falling so he must wait, his wish only that he could go back and return the bar to its delicate pegs. I feel this wish while watching a silent television alone in a city where the rain is falling like a failure that never stops coming down from the skies. I want to help him back up, the way I wanted to help Freud in the short movie about his flight from Vienna. His safe emptied by the Gestapo. The Swastika over his door. Then an old man beneath a blanket on a chair in the sun of France with just a year to live. He looked fallen. What I mean to say is Freud seemed to be waiting for something like a dream he once had to fall to earth beside him.

My Emptied Valise

This picture could rob many a man of his faith.

—Dostoyevsky

I am in Terezín and it is raining and cold,
the mud of the pathways inside the fort
as moist as the rooms built into the walls are humid

though tomorrow, the mud will dry to dirt
and the rooms will not

not ever—

Then the Lord sent a crow digging up the earth
so that he might show him
how he should cover the dead body of his brother.

The absence of electric lighting, the old wiring
either rotted away or dangerous

bare copper connected to naked throw switches
and single porcelain outlets that dangle from the ceiling

the doorways & windows
without shutters or panes

to stop the swallows arcing in and out
to tend their mud-daub nests
glued into the corner edges of the vaulted ceilings

like boxes in boxes of boxes.

Later the bus in Jerusalem blows up on the car radio
and the Zaka come with their scrapers and their trowels,
the pieces sorted and returned to relatives for burial.

So much I have loved your shadow,
that there now remains for me
nothing more of you.

The drowned man fished from the river
like a stiffened perch, his body

the model for the word on lips

removed and pressed upon
page after page

like a sticky kiss from a movie star, her indulgence
sold at the county fair as the five-dollar negative of sin,

so that what is death at first sight,
as they say, is life if you look within,
and vice versa, life is death

on squares of white paper, the blood-red
not the lips but what has spread upon them,

the kiss exchanged for gold,
the match exchanged for flame

slowly burning first what is dry
and then what has been moistened
by the breath—

Why has your countenance fallen?

the leather of my boots surrendering finally
to the present, the darkening seepage
working its way up each foot,

the movie star of my mind waving away the last customers,
blotting her lips with a napkin and stepping from the booth

to be blown up in a wide world of remembered misery,
forgotten misery and the kind of misery
that gets buried, then dug up and reburied

secretly on a hillside, in a valley, along the banks of a river,
overlooking a vast plain

where a farmhouse burns and the cattle lie dead and dying—

this real estate of the industry of aftermath,
this charcoaled realization

that graceful young men with guns are capable
of kicking overweight older women lying helpless,
      or already killed,
in the head.

Must a spatula in a lunch box
be a first tool for kindness?

If you will stretch forth your hand towards me to slay me,
I am not one to stretch forth my hand towards you to slay you.

Shrapnel sifted from guts with a colander.

He doesn't believe in God, and he talked
a good deal about it,
but all the while it appeared to me
that he was speaking outside the subject.

Safe inside my fort, my luminist
photographs the sodden light

pushing through doorways and window arches
like the snow from an avalanche in the mountains—

Right now I was sitting somewhere high up in the Pyrénées.

I am an idiot that I cannot see
where I am when I am
and dream only of where I am not—

You shall be a fugitive and a wanderer on the earth.

Am I interested merely in death and its astonishment?

140,000 taken to Terezín.
  33,000 died there.
  88,000 deported.

  19,000 residing at Terezín survived.
  3,000 deported survived.

Total deaths estimated at just under 120,000.
Of the 15,000 children, only 132 survived.

It remains with me to be a shadow among shadows,
To be a hundred times darker than the darkness.

Later, I enter the mausoleum of the Kunstmuseum
and stand in front of Christ entombed
feeling optimistic and invisible

thinking of the mysterious flesh but remembering

Caja des Visiones, Manuel Álvarez Bravo, 1938—

meaning I go,
pay my entry,
stare into the box—

the beard stiffly forsaken,
the finger broken at its source—

but recall the boy fallen from hunger
on the streets of Lodz, his hand up-reaching,
his body gone from him, he

knowing he is not going to make it.

Just having this photo
in a box in my house
makes my refrigerator obscene.

I look into it daily, throwing out
things gone moldy with forgetfulness,

romance and nostalgia,
a wilted carrot, some rotten grapes.

Another something explodes on a street corner
and another somebody comes apart at the seams.

To be as open as a black leather valise
turned upside down in the wind

He took his life in Port-Bou
the night after his arrival

Travel and you find
evil is cosmopolitan

torture, from Latin 'torquere,' to twist

meaning I found
it everywhere:

Sitting in a park in Prague, Pavel said to me, *No you still don't understand.*
See those two men sitting on that bench? The one on the right, maybe he is secret
police. And the one on the left, maybe he is dissident. Maybe he is in jail and
tortured by man on the right. Now they sit on same bench, feed same pigeon.
Silence. Jackdaws pulled trash from a bin, piece by piece. Then Ivo said,
That guy on the right. He is my father.

Oh shameless tourist of conscience,
little traveler to former hells

I have dreamed so strongly of you
I have walked so much, talked so much

would I
have survived

and how—

no wiring because there was never electricity,
no plumbing because there was never water,

no food because there was no one to be saved.

The boy crumpling to the ground, that boy
dying as surely as I would die,

thrown up against the insurmountable wall
of the end of his life—

Desnos moving through the ranks
of a group of the doomed, awaiting the gas chamber

reading their palms, predicting happiness and long life

red rose of typhus

a matter of days

lying back on a plank bed
in Terezín, then slipping away

his tin box of poems

a kiss from the lip of the mind

blowing up in me

I am floating like paper
caught in the updraft of ash

he was nobody

he was millions

a mound by the riverside

a place of no words no box no body

of no place remembered, forever

the shadow that will come and come again
into your sun-blessed life.

Boys Whistling like Canaries

If there was a mountain and then a mountain on the mountain,
then there would be a path that ran up to the base of that mountain
like the beginning of a story about a heaven.

And if there was a heaven, then there would be an island below it
green orange trees circling a red square full of singing canaries,
the flocks of boys beneath basking on sidewalks
dreaming like pigeons drowsing on rooftop edges
while waiting for someone
to drop a piece of sandwich onto the ground.

If only I could find my way down to this earth
then I could eat its food and remember
that when I was a young pigeon—

that when I was young,
I too was a pigeon, like you.

But this is not that story
because I was born out of doubt
seven months after my parents married each other
in a small church below the cliffs above the sea—

this is not that story
because I have been unable to believe in a heaven for years—

this story is about the note you hear
in the song of the canary just now,
a lightweight sound, a tiny breath
they learned from a boy not unlike that boy
whistling his way across the parched expanse of this square—

the Placa de Generalissimo

named for the general banished to this island that Bolívar left
in order to free the new world, the old one being already lost
to the madness of decrepitude and the false preservatives of nationalism.

But you must know, every man is a boy gone mad with age.

As mad as the botanical gardens planted here in 1788,
its seeds of enlightenment grown unnaturally.

No complexity of pattern and shade from its branches,
no careful art of pruning to entwine a riot of vegetation
into a diverse botany captured apart from nature

but a still and stagnant memento mori to landscape,
each plant a geriatric miracle of its species

perfectly spaced apart the precise width of the head gardener's leather shoe
allowing him to more easily eliminate unwanted vegetation
while bringing water each day around noon to pacify the rest.

These wide boulevards the generalissimo might embrace
as he did this *placa* lazily strewn with café tables and chairs,
his arms outstretched to demonstrate in his conspiracy the width
a full battalion might require to take a city's center on the march,

the first warmth of the morning tripping off the mountain's edge,
and the fog falling all the way down the hillside
to the sea and all the ships in port.

The head gardener was a man with no patience for generals.
He was a scientist and believed in the working man,

not because he had read Marx and Engels
or sung "L'Internationale" on the first of May,

but because his copy of *Das Kapital* was made hollow in the center
to hold a small glass bottle of homemade apricot brandy
stoppered with an ancient waxed cork wrapped in string—

my sweet dialectic he said—

retrieved from its place on a shelf in his small wooden office
stashed in a dark corner of the garden walls
where he and his assistants would begin each day with a coffee
cooked in a brass pot on a brazier and laced with the brandy
as antidote to the aches and pains that came with being part of reality—

that most men, in order to feed and shelter their families, have only their
      bodies to give in exchange.

And so I cannot blame the head gardener
for using his shoe to measure out the spacing of his plants
or for his lack of elegance when pruning his trees—

though his education might allow him different
he worked as hard as his men, his back bent to the shovel,
and dug down into the black soil like any grave digger
stolidly building a final home for himself.

His son was a boy who dreamed like the crow flies
with a jungle of limbs akimbo, flopping and squawking his way
through the house out onto the street and down the narrow steps

to the *placa* where the generalissimo sat ensconced upon his wobbly wire chair
halfway through his soliloquy of overthrow and redemption.

By now the boy was whistling

a tune everyone he passed felt was so familiar
they were surprised when they could not recall its name—

perhaps part Mozart, a bit of *jota*, a little flamenco
he might have heard one night over the small brown radio
his father kept stashed behind a cupboard in the kitchen,

or a piece of the music that wailed from the club with the green light
spilled from its doors late at night when the men stumbled out,

or the voice of his mother calling to him *come home small one*
or even the songs of the canaries that filled each tree
and every block in every town and village across this island
that was becoming every day more and more like a cage

and less like a step on a path at the base of a mountain
that led to a story of heaven tilting and gleaming at the edge of the sky.

But the tune in the boy's whistle does not matter
because truthfully, the boy was whistling no tune
except the one created by the contours of his unconscious,

the notes going precisely where he was going
and occupying exactly what he was thinking—

nowhere and nothing

like a canary perched at the top of its tree
its breast splitting open the sky with its lime-green,
singing the only tune that had ever been in its head.

This moment—

let it all rain down.

The heavens, the mountain, the story of how the path came to be.
Every hundred years, the mountain explodes,
the last in 1909.

Let's have an early one.

Better everyone die here—

the generalissimo in his wobbly chair,
the boy in his song, his father
the head gardener and his men
sipping dialectic and coffee from fertilizer cans—

than the million who would die afterwards.

But no, the generalissimo heard the boy whistling
and immediately knew this nothing
now rapidly effeminizing his country

as he was just telling his conspiracy gathered about him like flies

had to be stopped—

You must wrestle the law like an angel
to make it obey
God's will and not man's desire to be free.

And so he consigned the boy to his prodigious memory
to be recalled three years later and added to a list

written out carefully on the best paper
at a desk once owned by a king or a king's bastard son

by a secretary with a lisp who had never thought
she would get anywhere or any place so grand
without first removing her underclothes—

about which I can assure you, she was not wrong.

Later, the general would boast with pride,
his country had so many prominent intellectuals,
in so many cities the army had to use the football stadium
in order to kill them all.

Bullfighting rings being too small.

Except on the island, where the boy and his father

(because where would a boy get nothing from
if not from his own father?)

were led by the *guardia* to an empty banana warehouse
unilluminated except for the shafts of sunlight streaming
through rivet holes cut all around in the corrugated steel,
and pushed towards a group of men loitering at one end

neighbors, cousins and friends

all of them shivering though it was not cold.

Perhaps from nerves
or perhaps from the absence of nerves

the boy began to whistle

but this time
for the first time

he was not whistling a tune made of nothing
but the tune sung by the canary
trapped by the bird man with the small shop
downtown next door to the motorbike repair—

a canary who after years singing from the top of his tree
in the *placa*, found himself suspended in a small wire cage
with rust spots at each of its welds—

a cage nailed to the yellow wall of the shop
that the canary had just realized
would likely be his tomb—

this song of sudden mortality

was the one the boy whistled now.

It made the men of the *guardia*
go mad immediately,

and they shot them all, an entire warehouse of men,
in less than twelve minutes,

the boy hit first in the throat

so that he fell beneath a steadily growing pile
of men in great bunches,
the air so thick with smoke and explosions
and the cries of men dying calling out for each other
their wives and their children and God

you might have thought the volcano indeed was erupting.

Then silence
save a last breath escaping
through the hole in the throat of the boy.

How do you explain this sort of madness
except that it must come from the songs of the birds
as their last revenge for the cages of men?

Afterwards, the mother took her broom
and a chair from the café to the edge of the town

and began sweeping the earth
from one side to the other.

She started at the base of the mountain
and slowly worked her way up

walking backwards,
her footsteps disappearing

as her steady broom left behind
a smooth gray path in the volcanic soil

that her neighbors followed worriedly
urging her home, wringing their hands

asking her *what are you thinking,*
where are you going

only to receive each time the same answers

Of a heaven.

To meet Bolívar.

Until they finally stopped asking
and then they stopped going.

And then they started to forget.

When the mother finally reached the top
she set down her broom, set up her chair,
and made a black cup of coffee.
Then she sat down and waited
to disappear into thin air.

If there were a heaven, she would have found it then.
But if there wasn't, then she just rotted away.

And if there wasn't a heaven, then perhaps there wasn't a path.
And if not a path, then not a mountain or an island
or a town or a square or a boy.

If you like, I can confess that none of the details here are true,
a crime for which perhaps I should be shot,

but you cannot deny the canaries singing at the top of each tree.
And if there are canaries, consider whether each note

might not be a body
buried someplace

no one remembers,

except for that one note
you just heard a canary sing

right overhead—

a lightweight note, a tiny breath
that may only leave your body
through a hole in your throat.

Four Songs

Song #1

Rubber band around my wrist
round wristwatch
sundial baseball bundled string
no glove no glove oh
bat made from a tree
limb this morning I left home
hungry but my dream
a wrist watch playing shortstop
won't go away from me

Song #2

Papa papa papa

pa pa pa pa

papi papi papi

pa pi pa pi

Come home from where you are gone
so long I remember you
singing when I was asleep and little
so little I did not have teeth
but now I am big
as my eyes and I have
my teeth come home soon
papi bring me something sweet

Song #3

I have a tree that loves me
nobody loves me green leaf
tree loves me gray skin
trunk like an elephant's foot
when I wake up when I
am done with my work
I am sleepy sleepy
I climb the skinny my tree
loves me I have a tree leafy
loves me nobody loves me
like my tree not even
my grandmother's dead left foot.

Song #4

If I catch a lizard sleeping
if I find some fruit ripening
if I crack this shell open
if I find a shell to crack
if I hear a rifle
cracking if I see
a man in black walking
if I run I run I hide
I sleep if I catch a lizard
napping if I find some fruit
worth eating I eat I eat
I eat

here their son sits on the cool floor
nd studies English on a drawing that shows how to
tract gunpowder from shell casings and make a bomb
at will disable a Humvee if placed correctly

a road outside of Fallujah.

has never seen a Humvee.
has not seen his father in years.

thing but fists might be written on the wall.

in, *When they tear us limb from limb,*
will give them nothing but fists in return.

if it is, it is
written in English.

onimo said, *We heard that some white men*
measuring land to the south of us.

onimo said, *We could not understand them very well,*
e had no interpreter, but we made a treaty with them
aking hands and promising to be brothers.

onimo said, *Every day they measured land with curious instruments*
ut down marks which we could not understand.

oil well #7 in the Dammam Field comes up big for Aramco,
Kirkuk in 1927 flows directly into a pipeline that fuels 2003.

he brought me back to the door of the temple; and behold,
was issuing from below the threshold of the temple towards the east—

a ravine to a canyon that flattens into a saddle that becomes a pass
egin walking over on their way to the other hundred horizons,

a small spring flows out from between green limestone like a song.

Little Robe

Geronimo's ancestors left Asia early
so they would not discover gunpowder

and yet

it came for them
like any long lost son

to the middle of the middle of a desert
that was not yet Arizona
or white or even theirs

property being brought by gunpowder
as its first gift to its new home.

Later a slender man refills the minibar in a hotel room
He is sweating his way through his brown shirt
and is more than likely from Pakistan.

On the television, *Hogan's Heroes*.

He is in trouble for moving too slowly,
but he needs to be careful about his work.

He does not drink or read English
and must sort bottles by their colored labels.

Why so many green, so many red, and so few orange

He pauses to think of his wife, her *dupatta*
translucent in the smokeless light of afternoon
as she waits beneath a tree outside the madrasa

Syed Ahmed Khan typed in black on each of his paychecks, his finger
wet smudging the border of the blue Securi-Print paper
as he carries it to the Cash Al-Nitee at 2 AM
stepping over a drunk woman
who lost her homeland security too baby wanna fuck
and pays 25% to wire whatever remains to a street in Lahore.

Tonight he thinks his name is a cruel swindle.
His son thinks his name is a dream

mixed with water that remembers the light
and who had it in their eyes

not light like truth
but truth like water
in the desert after a rain
in the mountains

and how the Apaches hid for years in the hoodoos
waiting for the shot they hoped would come,

when the stagecoach slowed enough to become a Humvee.

Then Geronimo came out of the mountains to the desert floor
where he sat down to meet with a general named Crook
whom he understood perfectly even when he did not speak Apache.

Even when he did not speak.

Meanwhile in the shadows, a photographer named Fly
fumbled a little robe of black over his head,
his back to a wall of creosote and prickly pear,
his eyes wrestling each other to focus in the relative darkness.

Then he said, 'Let me go, for the day is breaking.'
But Jacob said, 'I will not let you go,
unless you bless me.' And he said to him,
'What is your name?'

Fly flicked a scorpion from a rock near his hip
and poured collodion and man-blinding nitrate
over a glass plate that somehow remained unbroken

long enough to record the look of men who knew
water not as given by God but as God himself

flowing from beneath the temple, wrestling with what
comes from the water, that crosses the bridge

and brings men to light beneath the red lamp of a darkroom.

Later howitzers came to be cruise missiles
but Apaches changed into helicopters not insurgents.

Khan came to believe his money was a pact with a devil,
that sweat was his soul slowly removed from his body by ounces
and that the helicopters scouring central Phoenix with their lights
took with them everything he had ever dreamed was true.

Why is it that you ask my name?

When the police officers stopped him, he was only walking home
after laundry, his papers in his apartment
so they would not be stolen from him by marauding bands.

His mouth as dry as guncotton.
His hip felt out of place.

They took a Polaroid of his soul.
They gave him bottled water.
They called him in on the radio.

His son never dreamed where they would put him.

Geronimo found himself grounded in Florida
chained to a no-fly list 1,500 miles long.

Later Fort Pickens became Guantánamo Bay.

And there he blessed him.

Little Robe, Son of Geronimo, Apache Chief,
killed September 10, 1885, age two years,
by a roving band of Mexican insurgents.

Later September 10 became what if.

When they tear us limb from limb,
we will be like water to their blood.

Then gunpowder became smokeless
through the addition of collodion and ether
and gunners could see targets more clearly
without the black clouds of exploding powder,

and targets became any war photographer after Fly.

Somehow over the unbroken hundred horizons
the glass plate remained Geronimo's face looking back sideways
as his people's land became unportable with property lines.

His son dead and buried within gun sight of the spring.

In whatever tribe the alien resides,
there you shall assign him his inheritance.

Ballistite, Cordite, Semtex and C-4.

Later water became oil not wine.

Four Angels

Gabriel

These are my hands, these are my feet.
I've had them all my life
and they have always been faithful.

In the morning, I say to my feet
today, we will go walking

to the barn, to the fields,
to the market with the crops.

My hands wash me.
Feed me.
Carry the rake, dig with the hoe,
pull the wagon from the barn
to the horse.

But my eyes betray me.

When I saw what I saw,
I said to my hands,
help them,
but my eyes said stay.

When I saw what I saw,
I said to my feet,
go to them,
but my eyes said run.

Now there is a place in my fields
I do not run through with the plow.

My feet will lead us there.
My hands will show us
where we must dig.

Michael

My brother is a lazy farmer, never
culling the weeds, never
sharpening the blade of his knife.

When the men came, they said
to him, We have killed your wife.
Now you must kill your daughters.

The night so dark,
the lantern had no power
against it, but I could see

a stain climb my brother's pants.

I knew he could not do it.
I knew his machete was not sharp.

They brought them out
still sleepy, rubbing their eyes
and blinking,

unsteady on their legs
like lambs in the spring.

The prayer I made
was not for myself.

Raphael

The air-raid sirens are like truth
spilled from a bucket at the top of a pole—

soon someone will be dead
or heavily wounded

and their house will be in flames.

You hear the doors of the neighborhood
open and close, slamming each way,

while underneath, your heart's pounding

as you grab the kids and shove
them down into the shelter

where you wait.

After, you go back upstairs
to finish with breakfast
or reading the paper—

nothing changes,
except for the dead.

I used to call my sister in New Jersey
to tell her we were okay,

but she'd just say,
Do you know what time it is here?
It's the middle of the night.

We were all asleep.

We are those whom God helps,
who sleep with the dead,

who collect fingers still clutching handbags
detached from their arms,

who scour the ceiling of the café
for the brain of a woman

caught in mid-dream

and fit a leg with a sock
to the hip of her child,

who carry the jellied torso
to its arms and its head

and wrap what's left of the bomber
and his shattered skin

in black plastic we deliver
to a woman who waits

in the doorway
of an emptying home.

There is
no reward.

(Men entered the back of the theater as silently as the ghosts of their fathers.)
(Afterwards the ghosts of our fathers licked the blood from their hands.)

Soliloquy of the Suicide Bomber

Every morning, the sun comes up
and the walls of my room begin to yellow with warmth—

I must not be a good man.

My friend says she made an agreement with God
and then her baby came.

How can you tell, I asked,
an agreement with God
from a pact with the Devil?

My head as full
as the seed splitting the olive
black as the green is green.

I wonder when
it will explode.

On Dogs & Urban Warfare

If a bird then a dog then another bird.
If food then the dog again and again.
If the sky then a gun and a hand
and a helicopter.
Oh helicopter, like a bird, then
another bird,
the dog's run off,
where's the food,
where's my gun,
when's that hand
pointing at the sky
going to go off
empty again
again.

Why Wrestle an Angel

The yellow dog is barking me awake
while the black dog eats both bowls
no matter how hard I shove his fat ass.

Why wrestle an angel?

The sun has yet to show the sycamores
how much more they need water
than I need a toy truck
in the pocket of my fading childhood memory

We are all mythmakers, storytellers, our beds of feathers
and horses chasing what is freer than we

A man lying in wait
sees an animal run behind a tree
and thinks *wait*

it is what comes out the other side that is the story.

When no animal appears, he must
become a better storyteller.

A general points to a small truck
that scoots 'cross a bridge
in southern Iraq
just before a laser-guided smart bomb

opens like the dressing gown of Azrael's
four thousand wings, licking
the eyes of the world
with the tongues of the world

the truck passed over the bridge,
then the bomb smote it.

Wagging and blinking, my dogs of war
buckle my knees as I open the screen door
to put the morning's spiderweb
across my stubbly face like a purloined veil
of chastity and innocence

not someone's house,

while the yellow dog humps the black dog
with the languid good humor
of two boys punching each other's shoulders
grinning and wincing, wincing and grinning

until the black dog drags the yellow dog
down into the creek by the folds of his neck.

Luckiest man in the world
says the general

and the press corps laugh with the world

vaporized in the cracked rearview
of a Deux Cheveaux hurtling to Baghdad
like a scarab running from the sun.

Carry me cross the River Jordan, I say,
to the dogs who are so soaked in it
they would be laughing too
if laughing was something dogs needed

to make sadness more bearable

or loss.

The man in the truck is dead,
the smart bomb's blast circle larger
than his truck is faster, thermobaric

pressure sucking out his eardrums,
then his lungs, then his heart,

the truck separating at all of its seams
as the fuel transforms his body's
loosening taffy into ethylene flame

that consumes two miles of oxygen
six feet off the ground.

This story will be the story that comes out
later,

the animal running from the other side of the tree,

because he has delivered me from all kings,
and because he has made me look down
on all my enemies.

A man wakes up one morning and feeds his dogs.
He loads his tools into his truck
and drives off humming, his dogs

barking each other silly beneath a yellow tree.

The sun is rising.
The air is cool.

As he crosses the bridge, he remembers the truck
he carried in his pocket when he was a boy
was just like the one he drives now,

the air from the vent circling his neck
under his shirt,

and he thinks

I am the luckiest man in the world

as sun hits the mirror
and he disappears into its light.

Some Truths Noted While Walking Alone

The triangular window holds its corners differently
than the square window.

The square window is open to suggestion.

The circular window is afraid
of what comes from the sky
and makes its view known simply.

The sky always dreams of a dress
made of yellow squares each night
but forgets the image entirely upon waking.

Blue then is the absence of memory.

The clouds are farm animals.

There is no pig.

Great Pickup Lines of the Twentieth Century

The red barn blue sky green trees and amber water spuming white over granite
as a minor league pitcher leans over a fence towards a girl with big teeth,

Your eyes are like Coca-Cola, he says.

This is an honest poem.

In 1909, Albert Kahn spent his fortune
on 72,000 *autochromes lumières,* a color process
made of starch rolled onto a glass photographic plate,

convinced people would not destroy
what they could see was made of flesh.

This was followed by World War I.

World War II.

And Kodachrome.

So much depends upon . . .

In 1966, Larry Burrows saw a colored man stagger
into the arms of another colored man
on a hilltop in a forest of slaughtered trees near Dong Ha,

only they were colored differently and no one was laughing
at the name of the place, the mud and blood thicker

than laughter

and dismemberment better than memory
at recalling what was torn from the body
and what was given back in carefully labeled bags.

Makes you think all the world's a sunny day . . .

On February 1, 1968, General Nguyen Ngoc Loan put a bullet
in the ear of Nguyen Van Lem and Eddie Adams made it black & white.

Still, color came out of Nguyen Van Lem's brain
and entered the mind of several million Americans,

who said in survey after survey
that blood sure looks like blood
when seen on an RCA.

His master's voice.

Then today in Jerusalem, a woman leaned into the window of a car
and a Katyusha rocket from the West Bank cut her in half,

the photographer angling to get not just the blood
but the body and the car flaming like a cauldron

dropped out of the sky into the forge of Hephaestus.

If you hear nothing, you had better get the fuck down.

My first camera was a Nikon, purchased
after seeing one slung around the neck of Tim Page
reclined in Vietnam like it was his sofa.

Even now, when I walk out into my backyard
I think of Vietnam, not because my backyard is a jungle—

I don't even have a backyard.

I live in New York City on East 96th Street
One grandfather was a minister,
the other, a surgeon—

a Presbyterian and a Lutheran.

So before me there was a belief in God,
and then a string of images I remember

flowing out of Vietnam like entrails
carefully unraveled from an opened body.

The Lutheran put men back together
on a hospital ship in the Pacific during World War II.

The Presbyterian spent the war in a prison camp
in Manila, Philippines, with his family.

I became a poet.

. . . a red wheelbarrow, glazed with rainwater, beside the white chickens.

Take a plane across the country a week after a major disaster
and look for Srebernica, Mogadishu, Banda Aceh

lodged in a Motel 6 of the national consciousness
and you'll find free coffee, a clean mattress
and all the donuts you can eat before the salesmen get up.

This is my backyard.

Take a photograph. It'll last longer.

Meanwhile, a boy leans through a low hole in a wall
to look at a group of American soldiers
carefully working their way up an alley in Sadr City

no wider than he is tall—

the hole placed perfectly for an IED.

Hey baby, come here often?

Longer and longer.

Overheard in an Airport

Nothing metaphoric about getting blown up.
The air explodes like a motherfucker,
then there are pieces of bodies
all over you, someone's brains and guts
and your blood on the ground.
Then if you're lucky, they come right away,
put you in an ambulance
and take you to a hospital
where they cut off your clothes,
start swabbing you down and sewing you up.
Someone pulls a finger out of your pants,
so they count yours
8, 9, 10
twice
8, 9, 10
then throw it away.

Hung like an Owl on a Barbed-wire Fence

≈

Hwy. 80, near Rodeo, Arizona

The dust plume from the truck rises in the distance like a gown
on a woman rising slowly from a bed, her quilt of brittle bush yellow
tumbling through the window light streaming over the Peloncillo Mountains
down upon the floor of the San Simon valley,

while the ferrous red rock of Portal Peak and the walls of Horseshoe Canyon
sit tinctured by the lemon of lichen and the bone white of raven's nests
lodged in the hollows of sandstone worn out by wind—

the strange relation of distance and time in a flat land:

objects approaching from great distances
can be seen hours before they arrive,

Tuesday seemingly visible from Monday
and Monday spent straightening up

to look beyond the unsteady creosote
and see how much closer whatever has gotten,
then bending back to whatever else—

the sand in the motor on the pump, the thorn
in the bend of the hose, the post on the fence
gone lazily over to one side
due to termites, dry rot and the boredom of cattle—

everything taking forever to reach finally through distance
and yet everything just as slowly going away
as if nothing is ever actually here—

except the sand, the thorn, dry rot—

and time itself is a body
that sits beside you on the porch
and lays down beside you at night
when the desert becomes a great neuronal sheet
of fireflies the nighthawks eat one by one on the wing—

the truck now close enough to see its color of a winter bluebird,
the paint worn through with the rust of unpainted metal
pockmarked and burned by the sun,

and what appears at first to be a sock flapping from the roof
is instead a boy of about ten or twelve, standing,

his hands gripping the frame of the cab
while turning to check the dog
asleep on a feed sack against the gate of the bed.

When the truck reaches the end of the dirt, it stops
then lurches forward against first gear,
pushing itself onto the smooth surface of Hwy. 80 north,

the asphalt insubstantial beneath the heavy tires
after the corrugations of the grated dirt,
and they roll north towards Rodeo as if suddenly

untethered, a feeling the boy loves more than any other,

even that of his mother leaning down each evening,
her skin blue-white in the cool dark of his room,
to kiss his forehead and push back his hair with her hand.

If she were here, he would be made to sit inside.
But on these early morning runs, his father lets him be,
and the boy shifts his boots, hooking each tattered toe
beneath a cleat bolted to the floor of the bed

and spreads his arms as any boy might do,
the wind catching the neck of his shirt,
snapping his clothes, nearly ripping them apart

at the seams, his body twisting
into and out of balance,

as the truck carries him along
as near to flight as a boy

standing alone in the back of a truck
with a sleeping dog and his arms out wide

may ever be.

≈

Najaf, Iraq

After six days of heavy fighting,
of tanks and helicopter gunships pounding the neighborhood

as unseen men dash between houses and over rooftops
carrying a clatter of rifles and RPGs,

even the birds look different—

sacred ibis curl back over the palms like a squadron of A-10s

and the bulbul that nests each year in the neighbor's tree
sticks the clack of a safety into his song—

even a stray moment of peace is changed

by strange blooms of orange fire
as a small herd of black & white goats
panics in the middle of a minefield,

and a man walking down the sidewalk
looks like a soldier or a sniper

or a bomb

at a distance, changing even

a father,

who slips out into a lull between firefights,
thinking of apricots but also bottled water
and flour and fresh batteries and a few paper bags of pistachios,

his son chasing along like a mouse
changed too,

smarter, more wary
about what comes after
being left behind.

Perhaps the fighting has already restarted,
the *pock pock pock* of small arms
followed by the seismic *foomphs* of mortar rounds

walking their way through the city
as the gunners shoot adjust and repeat,

the father reaching back to grab his son's hand,
and pull him around the next corner

where the unending dun of the road widens
into a U.S. patrol uncoiling razor wire
around some men who sit on the ground,

their hands bound with zip-ties, their heads
covered with black nylon bags—

bowed down so low in the desert
even the wind seems tall, the infinite hues of the dirt

and the dark familiarity of another black bag, another a zip-tie,

now put on the father but carried by the son

inside

like a second body, or the memory
of a body floating facedown in the reeds—

the boy left standing alone, boys not yet
considered to be anything but boys,

his eyes as big around as an owl's
lost mid-flight in the lights of a car
careening through a desert night.

And the boy is screaming, like the owl
would be screaming, death come fast upon him

like the light in the fire on the blade of the knife
that came upon Isaac bound in his own sticks,

his father's hand taken from him
and made into ash,

his world burning in his eyes,
the sand sliding from beneath his feet

as a Blackhawk flies close support overhead,
his small voice swallowing its spiral whine
and spitting it back skywards,

until the shutters on the houses start to rattle
and the doors start to shake, as if next
the graves in the vast graveyard to the north

might open and answer the boy's bloodless notes
with ones of their own—

the men in their hoods shifting and nodding,
the soldiers sweating straight through their gear—

each thinking how open this space is, how
exposed they are now,
how many snipers they have already heard—

forever pulling itself to pieces
until the protective coating of distance
peels away like a skin

and nothing exists
that isn't a bullet
that isn't a gun sight
that isn't the smoke trailing out
a hole under the arm that leads to the heart.

And what leads more quickly to the heart
than a bullet

or a boy
who will become a bullet
hidden in the dance of the lark

crossing the path the bullet will take?

Finally someone picks up the boy,
someone pulls back the wire, someone
cuts the ties that bind the father's wrists,

and the boy folds into his father like a wing
as he gently pushes his hair back
with his hand

whispering,

Listen, small one,

we are floating, you and I, over palm trees
and rooftops towards the apricot sun.

There is nothing beneath us,
nowhere we can't go,

except that we will go there together,
always like this.

≈

Hwy. 80, near Rodeo, Arizona

The boy pounds the roof of the truck with his palm, stopping
his father who has not seen what the boy saw

something

white, hung like a skin

on the rusted barbed-wire line clotted with cow hair
running along the ditch like a coyote on a road,

the truck idling then grinding into reverse
with a growling complaint—

a road, a wide open plain,

Brewer's sparrows singing from the tops of blue sage
in the vague heat of the early morning desert sun

and then this barn owl dangling from the fence by its wing,

the bird's preternatural whiteness
seemingly both body and shroud—

then it moves

and the boy is everything
and nothing

until he is there, looking down at the thin band of a tendon
looped over the point of a barb and stretched
from the joint in the bone of the wing,

the owl hissing, its feet dangling
and dangerously sharp.

The father watches his son wipe his hands on his jeans,

then grab the wrists of the owl with a one-hand sweep,
lifting and turning the wing with the other

while narrowly avoiding the hook of the beak,

until the owl sits blinking and upright, its drooped wings
drawn slowly up to each side, its head swiveling level

collected, unperturbed,

as if the hand beneath could be so quickly forgotten,
and the sun's burning over the boy's shoulder

not the enemy

but a love so infinitely seductive,
those without antidote must hide from the blindness
that comes from its light—

the urge to hold tightly in one's hand
a thing without fear
without fear of one's own
and then to hold it a bit longer, a bit more tightly
still—

then the father,
both hands in his pockets,
says quietly
from the shoulder of the road,

Now let it go.

And the boy settles
and turns,

then holds the bird
over his head

and opens his hand.

≈

Najaf, Iraq

In the ochre haze of a distant dust storm
mixed with equal parts setting sun

a barn owl hovers over a field of razor wire
spun around an oil-pumping station,

then drops down
into the brambles of steel

reemerging
with a mouse in its beak

rising

as if by levitation
or strings.

Four Voices

They came on motorcycle, the motor buzzing
the heat the day made inside my head.

Then he was lying in the street, stretching out
his arm for something I could not see.

There was dust on his lips
he did not wipe away.

I was sleeping, then there was fire
bright as brought by the archangel Michael—

the metal roof flapping open, crying
like a baby lost among the stars,

until I realized it was a baby
blown upwards into the limbs of the tree.

I saw my neighbor running fast
through the alley, his eyes white

as the bone of a cow
left too long in the sun without rain.

I used his name, but he did not reply.
Already he was no longer the man I called out to.

We found them bundled like floats
from a net, clumped in the eddy

where the creek enters the river.
The fish had eaten away at the parts

they had been given by God. At first, we thought
they were pigs. Then we saw there were many others.

Faggot

A fragment of wood cracked off an axe handle

by the shock of the head hitting concrete,

a bright blue-orange spark like a flint's *chock*

chock, then a pile of slender sticks, a bundle of

cedar kindling, whittled-down pine slats

still sticky with pitch, a cracked baseball bat,

a fence post left over from range work,

an end chewed off by cattle and wrapped

in barbed wire with an eyelet inserted

to secure a chain to the gate,

a plywood Stop sign shattered with a tire iron,

then a waterproof match popped into flame like a word,

that word, tossed on top like the Great Unextinguishable,

eating first one limb, then another, and another,

oh how willing are the kiln-makers, how lonely

the water-carriers sprinting uphill from the creek,

their buckets spilling water in the moonlight

like silver dripping from the teeth.

Fluorescent Light

A boy in a hallway punches a girl in the arm, the sound like a wet sock falling into the bathtub, the hallway full of lead paint's pale green light hovering over the black linoleum the girl knows by heart, every scratch the janitor's spade made scraping old gum etched into her walk from fourth grade math to a third grade classroom where she'll wait in the hallway with a boy who is as brutal as she is brilliant at numbers, as if someone just put a hot steel ring in his nose with a pair of pliers, knowing how bright his pain would be and how little he would be able to understand about it, except that it could be inflicted upon another again and again, his fist pounding her arm, dulling her brilliance into something as ugly as fluorescent light, their constant hum like flies in the ears, the time like slow suffocation beneath a wool blanket each morning, why go to school to be beaten, why stay at home to grow darker, why every day he forgets himself, why she remembers him forever.

World of Mirth

—in memory of the Harveys

I once lost a dollar
in their store's
photo booth.

I was disappointed
but not unhappy.

My wife might have
even been laughing

at me or
with me,

one or
the other.

After all, things
worth more than a dollar
go missing
every-
day.

A family in a basement,
tape bound, throats slit,
then set on fire.

What dreams are lost to us now?

Watching *Hogan's Heroes* in German

When I'm watchin' my TV
And a man comes on to tell me
How white my shirts can be.
Well he can't be a man 'cause he doesn't smoke
The same cigarettes as me.
                                        —The Rolling Stones

Bob Crane's got his pants off and his camera
raised, the girl's ass pasted to his hips,

her straight legs muscled like a Vargas model
with a Bob Crane somewhere inside.

What exactly was he doing in there?

I am lying on a couch in Prague
sipping codeine and nursing a cracked rib
from coughing, my wife gone

looking for America again, our apartment bare-boned
except for me, a couch, and a television,

all German voices over American reruns,
the canned audience, American too,

laughing with me
though neither of us

speak German, for all we know

every *ja ich* perhaps a cruel joke on us,
the classic American paranoia, I think,
that every foreign language begins:

Two stupid Americans walk into a bar and . . .

I hear German every day, and each time
I think *Nazis!*
even though I am not a Jew.

Wer bin ich?

Right now, I am mostly made of codeine
but I am also American-made television,

the martial fife of *Hogan's Heroes*
in my blood like a thinner
understanding of the red-white-and-blue world

where Americans dupe the Devil with one-liners,
tunnels to town, dynamite and *Frauen mit den grossen Brüsten*

while outside it is 1970, King and the Kennedys are dead,
Marvin Gaye is beginning to wonder what's going on,
and the spinal injury of Vietnam paralyzes
even the stupidly nationalistic
with indiscriminate violence—

but no, I am here in Prague, only a few years before
you read this, lying on a couch
as Hogan speaks fluent German with Klink
who smiles as if the other side won

and I think for a moment
I might need to check the locks on the door

lest the SS come looking for my wife,
until I remember she is safe in New York City,

eine jüdische Stadt, lob Gott,

then Schultz, a Jew who escaped Austria
to become an overweight actor in Los Angeles,

*jawohl*s to Klink, a *Halbjude* who fled Germany
as a boy to take the reins of Stalag 13 as a man,

who stands next to Hogan's quiet American
wise-ass dreamboat
lost in the light of Jews playing Nazis

with a humor at once joyous and dark,
the skits of Purim danced on the executioner's footprints.

Aber sie sprechen Deutsch hier, Schatz!

So wrong in my ear, a tongue burning
like napalm on the body of Kim Phuc Phan Thi

who ran out of the flames towards me
one evening and forever naked and holy
a year after *Hogan's Heroes* ended.

She looked like a girl in my class
and burned
like any girl would have burned,

as we began to scare ourselves
first with My Lai, then Kent State,

a new television in every home
and in every new television,

the new color of blood
running red on jungle green,

washing away years of black & white victory
in early newsreels before a Saturday matinee,

leaving only the flickering presence of Super 8
in the low light of a pine-paneled den

of iniquity, Bob Crane shimmering
towards an ass spread like a history book
that reads:

After 1945, the United States started fucking
anything, anytime, anywhere—

Air America, Operation Condor, Iran-Contra:

Who am I?

I am afraid stilettoed naked women
sporting Mickey Mouse boob jobs
will insert weapons of mass destruction
into the wrong orifices and we'll all end up fucked,

German late-night television porn
having replaced Shultz and Klink

and 4 million dead Vietnamese
by a growing list of Iraqis
who swim in this Euphrates of codeine
that thins my blood just now.

I feel like I have lost that piece
of Bob Crane inside me forever.

Bin ich dieses Land?

Est-ce que je suis ce pays?

Do you come here often?

If the Jews played Nazis,

maybe Bob Crane was America

played by something much darker,

each covert operation slowly peeling back layers,
false flag of comedy to pure truth of porn,

the get it up, take it off, get it all down
on tape, baby, the money shot, the full facial,

the crème de la crème—

losing for years a piece of himself
in each one of his viewers,

then spending the last days of his life
trying to get it all back

with his dick.

Birdwatching at Yaxchilan

The afternoon after the curassow, a helicopter

with a government minister
from Guatemala
looking for his son,

a kayaker on the Usumacinta
three weeks late for dinner—

Nobody, we haven't seen
any bodies in the river

today—

That night, the URNG serenaded
teenage Mexican soldiers
from across the river

with the screams of jaguars
they'd learned by sleeping light,

tracer bullets arcing
overhead
like hummingbirds
fighting in the heat of midday.

Later in Lagos de Montebello
the children of refugees

showered us with flowers
then threw rocks at our car

as we left.

To the Boy at Lake Petén Itzá

Come back.
I'd like to see your fish,

small and gray, swimming
in a white plastic bucket.

You spent twenty minutes
still as a bittern

standing in the shallows
to catch it,

not for me.

Notes

p. 6, "Natalka": Thank-you to Gabriela Brauchli for her excellent translations of the Czech language sections in this poem.

p. 9, "Rain Coming Down like a Death of Angels": This poem contains excerpts from a letter written by Werner Heisenberg to his wife, Elisabeth, during his visit to Niels Bohr in September of 1941.

p. 12, "Operation Anthropoid": The title refers to the secret mission by Czech paratroopers on May 27, 1942, to assassinate Reichsprotektor Reinhard Heydrich, the success of which led to reprisals by the Nazis, including the complete elimination of the Czech town of Lidice and the murder of the town's men, women, and children. The poem commemorates Jindriska Novakova, who, at her mother's direction, moved a paratrooper's bicycle, leading in part to the entire family's arrest and deportation to Mauthausen, where they were exterminated on October 24, 1942.

p. 13, "In Which Freud Leaves Vienna and Goes Instead with Moses to London": Several of the excerpts in this poem are from Sigmund Freud's *Moses and Monotheism*, as well as from the Book of Exodus in *The New Oxford Annotated Bible with the Apocrypha, Expanded Edition*, edited by Herbert G. May and Bruce M. Metzger (New York: Oxford University Press, 1973).

p. 23, "My Emptied Valise": Excerpts in this poem come variously from the story of Cain and Abel as presented by the M.A.S. Abdel Haleem translation of *The Qur'an* (New York: Oxford University Press, 2004); a poem attributed to Robert Desnos and a line from William Kulik's introduction, both from *The Selected Poems of Robert Desnos*, translated by William Kulik and Carolyn Forche (New York: Ecco Press, 1991); a selection from *The Idiot*, by Fyodor Dostoyevsky; Lisa Fittko's account of conducting Walter Benjamin across the Pryénées in 1940, as presented in Howard Eiland and Kevin McLaughlin's translation of Benjamin's *The Arcades Project*, edited by Rolf Tiedeman (Cambridge, Mass.: Belknap Press, 1999); a line from Jean Améry's *At the Mind's*

Limits: Contemplations by a Survivor on Auschwitz and Its Realities,
translated by Sidney Rosenfeld and Stella P. Rosenfeld (Bloomington:
Indiana University Press, 1980); and a selection from Susan Sontag's
Regarding the Pain of Others (New York: Farrar, Straus and Giroux,
2003). The painting referred to in the poem is Hans Holbein's *Christ
Entombed.*

p. 55, "Little Robe": This poem contains excepts from *Geronimo: The Man,
His Time, His Place,* by Angie Debo (Norman: University of Oklahoma
Press, 1982), as well as passages from the Book of Ezekiel and the Book
of Genesis in *The New Oxford Annotated Bible.*

p. 84, "Hung like an Owl on a Barbed-wire Fence": This poem began with
a photo taken by AP photographer Jean-Marc Bouju of a father and
son who were being held by U.S. forces in An Najaf, Iraq, March 31,
2003. The boy, separated from his father by razor wire, began to scream.
Bouju's photograph shows the boy being comforted by his father after
being allowed into the enclosure by the soldiers. The father is wearing a
hood. The photo won World Press Photo of the Year in 2003.

p. 105, "Faggot": This poem was written in memory of Matthew Shepard, a
gay man murdered in Fort Collins, Colorado, on October 12, 1998. It was
composed after voters in Virginia approved an amendment to the state
constitution in 2006 that banned gay marriage.

p. 108, "Watching *Hogan's Heroes* in German": Thank-you to Jennifer
Nelson for her translations of the German passages in this poem, as
well as for her superb editorial suggestions throughout the original
manuscript.

Acknowledgments

The following poems are included in the chapbook *All About the Blind Spot and Other Poems* (Popular Ink, 2007): "Atas Ptáků," "Losing the World Championships," and "On Dogs & Urban Warfare."

"Atlas Ptáků" also appeared in *Hayden's Ferry Review*.

"Overheard in an Airport" appeared online at *Indelible Kitchen*.

"Great Pickup Lines of the Twentieth Century" appeared in *War Papers: Poetry 2*, compiled and edited by Halvard Johnson (Big Bridge Press).

"Some Truths Noted While Walking Alone" and "World of Mirth" appeared in *La Fovea*.

≈

Thank-you to David Brauchli, whose vivid, firsthand descriptions of the sounds of being under fire in a war zone found their way into several of these poems.

I would also like to thank the Virginia Center for the Creative Arts and the Vermont Studio Center for residencies used to complete work on this manuscript.

My love and thanks to my wife, Claudia, without whose help I would remain impossible.

And, finally, this book is dedicated to my dad. He took me outdoors.

About the Author

 Jorn Ake began as a painter, graduating from the College of William and Mary with a BA in fine arts. Ten years later, he moved to Arizona to complete an MFA in creative writing at Arizona State University. His first collection of poems, *Asleep in the Lightning Fields*, won the 2001 X. J. Kennedy Poetry Prize and was published by Texas Review Press in 2002. Popular Ink released a chapbook of his work, *All About the Blind Spot and Other Poems*, in 2007, and his second full-length collection, *The Circle Line*, is forthcoming from The Backwaters Press. He began writing *Boys Whistling like Canaries* in Prague, where he lived for three years. He currently lives in New York City.